POWER OF THE BOARDROOM

POWER OF THE BOARDROOM

REDEFINING LIFE'S PRIORITIES
ONE WOMAN'S MEMOIR

RHONDA B. GAINES, MA

POWER OF THE BOARDROOM © copyright 2015
by Rhonda B. Gaines. All rights reserved. No part of this book may be
reproduced in any form whatsoever, by photography or xerography or by any
other means, by broadcast or transmission, by translation into any kind of
language, nor by recording electronically or otherwise, without permission
in writing from the author, except by a reviewer, who may quote brief
passages in critical articles or reviews.

Scripture quotations taken from the *New American Standard Bible*®,
Copyright © 1960, 1962, 1963, 1968, 1971, 1972, 1973, 1975, 1977, 1995
by The Lockman Foundation. Used by permission.

ISBN 13: 978-1-940014-29-6

Library of Congress Catalog Number: 2014946294

Printed in the United States of America
First Printing: 2015
19 18 17 16 15   5 4 3 2 1

Cover and interior design by James Monroe Design, LLC.

Wise Ink, Inc.
Minneapolis, Minnesota

www.wiseinkpub.com
To order, visit www.itascabooks.com or call 1-800-901-3480.
Reseller discounts available.

*To Michael: Your obedience to God
has rewarded us with continual generational blessings
for our family to come!*

Success is not to be measured by the position reached in life as by the obstacles he has overcome while trying to succeed.

—Booker T. Washington

CONTENTS

Preface | xi

Introduction | 1

CHAPTER 1:
The Miracle—A Renewed Sense of Purpose 9

CHAPTER 2:
A New Perspective on Career 23

CHAPTER 3:
A New Mentor 37

CHAPTER 4:
A Newfound Respect for My Husband 53

CHAPTER 5:
Discovering the True Purpose of Family. 67

CHAPTER 6:
Preparing Children to Succeed in Life 77

Conclusion | 87

Acknowledgements | 93

Request to my readers | 95

PREFACE

The Power of the Boardroom—Redefining Life's Priorities

"The important work of moving the world forward does not wait to be done by perfect men."
—George Eliot

"Be strong and courageous!"
—Joshua 1:9

If you are inspired to read this book, then I believe that you have been chosen to be a leader of change by divine inspiration. Let me begin by saying that *The Power of the Boardroom* is a new strategy to think differently about our commitment to family and our careers. I wrote *The Power of the Boardroom* to challenge and redefine "success." Many of us, myself included, do all the right things. We dream big, pursue our career paths, and earn our professional accolades. Some of us aspire to have a seat at the boardroom table. By boardroom I don't mean an enormous conference room with all the grandeur afforded up-and-coming executives sitting around a table, leaning back in their executive chairs awaiting your contribution—although many of us do aspire to this. Rather, I believe that the "boardroom" has become a symbol for us as professionals. What we want as we climb the corporate ladder is esteem, respect, and to feel that our hard work is paying off. There is power in having a pinnacle for success that once reached means you've made it. We all have a benchmark and for years we plan to achieve that benchmark at all costs within our minds. Maybe, for some, the benchmark is an actual seat at a boardroom table. For me it was financial security to help afford the image that I was creating. I wanted to be respected and well known for my achievements.

The "boardroom" I created for myself was unhealthy. It looked wonderful at first glance—there was cachet and glitz. It was perfect for the Rhonda who justified the importance of putting career before family to accomplish her goals. The boardroom I desired placed more value on worldly success than on peace of mind and balance.

PREFACE

I wrote this book to challenge and encourage you—the aspiring executive—to become more than a success story among your peers and in your industry. You can be more. You can be an influencer of change in our corporate culture by redefining how we bridge faith and purpose within our careers. Your faith can be a gentle reminder at work about humility, the strength of good character, and the powerful impact that your career can truly have on your family and in your community. What would happen if you boldly brought your faith to the forefront of your professional and personal wants? What would you do differently if transparency and spiritual fortitude guided your steps? As you travel with me, please allow the voice of God to minister to your heart and determine if it is your time, as a servant leader, to help redefine life's priorities, and return the power of influence and harmony in our homes and community to God. It is time for committed leaders to help make the transformation a reality. Thank you for accepting the challenge and welcome to the team!

INTRODUCTION

The Masquerade

"When life gives you a hundred reasons to cry, show life that you have a thousand reasons to smile."

—Unknown author

"Because in much wisdom there is much grief, and increasing knowledge results in increasing pain."

—Ecclesiastes 1:18

For many years I could not see the joy in my circumstances because I was too focused on what I didn't have rather than the blessings in front of me. I was what you would call a "glass half empty" believer. My problem? I was living two different worlds: the world of reality and the world of the "successful" professional image that I was committed to creating. It would take me years to appreciate the Philippians 4:11 scripture, "For I have learned to be content in whatever circumstances I am."

I desperately needed encouragement to balance life and I desperately turned to self-help books as a first resource and the Bible as a secondary resource—if time permitted. When Michael, my husband, would suggest that I listen to Christian radio programs or ask if I'd join him in Bible study, I had mixed emotions. I would either do it reluctantly, feeling good for a short amount of time, or resort back to my comfort zone—trying to take control of my situation and solve my problems. I futilely searched for the bestseller of the moment, hoping to discover the latest self-help trend. I learned every strategy I could to help balance my career and family. But the harder I looked, the more challenges I faced as I juggled and strived to have it all.

I'm not blaming the self-help books. The problem was that I was more interested in quick answers and trying to find the "secret" through someone else's journey rather than being inspired by scripture and prayer. The stress of endless searching in the wrong places unexpectedly took its toll on my health and the quality of my life, which eventually caught up with me. The worst part was facing the harsh reality of being unable to conquer my stress. I could no longer push through it to mask my discomfort. I was in denial. To justify my denial, I convinced myself that my declining

INTRODUCTION

health and emotional turmoil was a small stumbling block and that I could still strive to reach my career goals regardless of the circumstances. I convinced myself that focusing on my career and achieving professional success was the most important priority in my life and that it was going to pay off in the end. I felt trapped in a body that wasn't mine for many years. The only thing I had left was my small window of façade to hold me over for one more hour, then one more day, until things got better. Even as my health declined, I continued working, keeping up a front by encouraging other career-minded women in my circles to prioritize their family's needs over their careers, knowing full well that I was doing the opposite.

I confidently touted my personal philosophy as the gospel. When young women would ask me how to have it all, I'd proudly profess, "You plan for success. Success does not plan for you!" I believed that by looking out for other women, I was cutting a deal with God, hoping that He would honor my intentions—although half-hearted—and perhaps change my own circumstances. Now I know that negotiating with God is futile. My approach was not biblical or smart on my part.

To make matters worse, I had a skewed perspective of successful role models and tended to lean toward trusting the advice of businessmen. Even though men in my circles were highly respected for their ability to create "wealth," in reality, many of their achievements happened at the expense of neglecting their families.

As I quieted my neuroses long enough to look at what I was doing to myself, I soon realized that I was in the exact state I had warned others about. Though I wanted desperately to change, I continued to mask my anxiety. I continued the masquerade. The more I continued to pretend that everything was fine, the more scared and disillusioned I became. I was especially fearful of how my choices were affecting my health, marriage, and children. I felt boxed in with nowhere to turn. I craved an identity that I could hold onto, but I felt my life slipping away.

Finally, I played my last hand. One night like so many others, I could not sleep and arose around 2 a.m. I did what I always did on nights like this—I got on my computer and tried to work. Though I was tired, I couldn't rest or think clearly. I felt strange and weak. I remember getting up and moving to the couch, hoping that might help. As I sat there, I began to cry for reasons I couldn't put my finger on and the tears didn't stop. I couldn't talk coherently to anyone for two days. The masquerade had finally ended.

My whole world had turned upside down. I was lost, scared, and felt so alone. As much as Michael loved

INTRODUCTION

me, he barely managed to take care of the kids and go to work—both a full-time job in and of themselves. He tried to offer as much support as possible, but I could sense his need for me to snap out of it so he could have the "ol'" Rhonda back.

That hopelessness went on for what seemed like a lifetime. After many years of searching for answers from doctors and counselors, trying different medications and lifestyle adjustments, my doctors determined that I would never work or function at the same level as before. My career was my identity for so long that to hear I would no longer have a career was devastating. During this dark period in my life, I learned how to operate in survival mode. Sometimes I would ask myself how the pressures of balancing my career with family, which had started out as fun and provided a sense of accomplishment and value, had morphed into something I could no longer control or manage. For the first time, I tasted defeat.

When I came to the realization that something had to change, I finally looked deep within and made tough decisions about my future. Even though pursuing medical help was the right response, it did not yield the outcome that I anticipated or needed. At the onset of my depression, I had no idea what the answer to discovering joy again would be, but I was absolutely sure that I had to try something different. After months of searching for answers through prayer, I had a breakthrough. God responded to me with grace in the midst of my hopelessness. What I heard and experienced could not be called anything less than a miracle.

If you're like me, when looking for a miracle you probably pray and fast for deliverance only to feel as if God isn't moving fast enough. It's not uncommon to doubt God. Even though we want to seek God's will and operate on His timetable, often as Christians we lose our focus in the process of waiting for His guidance. We begin to second guess His purpose and plan for our lives and to make decisions based on what we think God is doing rather than waiting to see His will unfold. For me it was difficult to wait on God. As long as I'm moving, I have semblance of control. But I quickly learned that moving without God by my side, under the pretense of His backing, is yet another masquerade. I leaned on a scripture as a starting point from Philippians 4:12: "I know how to get along with humble means, and I also know how to lie in prosperity; in any and every circumstance I have learned the secret of being filled and going hungry, both of having abundance and suffering need. I can do all things through Him who strengthened me." Though I was not at the "can do" part yet, I came to a point where I finally

INTRODUCTION

began working on being strengthened.

My miracle came from trusting God and through the obedience of developing an active personal prayer life and bible study with my husband, which I believe saved my life. During difficult times in your life, have you ever heard a small voice in your heart leading you in a certain direction? The peace derived from walking in His spirit and in His will is amazing. It becomes so easy to be thankful and to give God glory. But what about the quiet times when you are unable to hear His voice and completely know His will? Have you ever doubted God's purpose and plan for your life in the midst of your trials? Have you ever felt like hope and deliverance were impossible?

In the chapters that follow, I explore how overcoming several life obstacles strengthened my faith in God and how I finally came to experience the joy of His perfect will, purpose, and plan for my life without doing things my way. My journey of overcoming doubt, anger, and shame will hopefully illustrate the marvelous delight of God's grace and perfect peace. It took a total of seven years to accept how God miraculously restored my health, faith, family, and career. My faith restored joy to my life again without fear of failure. I began to love and enjoy my family as we rebuilt everything that we had lost in our journey—a failed business, marital strife, failed health, military deployment, bankruptcy, an overwhelming mound of college expenses for three children, and the death of several close family members. My story is truly a miracle of faith—a total gift to me in the most difficult, lonely period in my life. I learned that all circumstances in life, however painful, are especially designed to help lead us down the path to having a closer relationship with God and to experience the true gift of hope that only He can provide. Then and only then can we really start living life to the fullest.

CHAPTER 1:

The Miracle—A Renewed Sense of Purpose

"The only thing that stands between a man and what he wants from life is often merely the will to try it and the faith to believe that it is possible."

—Richard M. DeVos

"To you it was shown that you might know that the Lord, He is God; there is no other besides Him."

—Deuteronomy 4:35

Can you remember your last personal crisis—a moment in your life when you hit a wall and couldn't see the forest for the trees? If you think about it, many of the most useful inventions and solutions were developed in response to an insurmountable crisis—research for the cure of cancer through the Susan G. Komen movement; improved communications through new technology of the Internet; social media and mobile devices and improved medical health care devices for heart and kidney transplants, to name a few. Through the years, I've come to learn that if the perfect storms of our lives didn't exist, we'd probably not be as motivated or as resourceful. The most insurmountable crisis of my life—recovering from burnout and depression—presented me with two options: I could become a fighter or I could become a victim. Before this realization, I initially handled depression by becoming dependent on my husband. I willingly left my well-being in his hands as I became unable to make the most simple life decisions. However, unexpectedly after September 11th, my husband, who was a Navy Chief reservist, was notified that he had to leave for active duty in response to our national crisis. The military gave him twenty-four hours to notify his family and employer as he prepared for deployment.

Life for me moved from difficult to virtually impossible. The inability to communicate with my husband for months on end was a challenge. Now that I was a single mom, I had to ask for help from the person closest to me—my oldest son, who at that time was a junior in

THE MIRACLE—A RENEWED SENSE OF PURPOSE

high school. I began to push most of the family responsibilities onto him. I still wasn't coping very well with the daily activities of raising children. Three months into my husband's deployment, the reality of how my decisions had negatively impacted my family became too hard for me to ignore. One afternoon after picking up my children from school, I made them dinner, and then could barely make it up the stairs to my bedroom. As I ended my prayers that night and drifted asleep, there was a gentle knock at my door. As the door opened, a soft voice called, "Mom. Mom." The voice belonged to my oldest son. When I opened my eyes, I found him trembling with tears streaming down his face. He spoke slowly, deliberately, and almost apologetically. He said, "Mom, I am not Dad. I can't do this anymore."

At that moment my life flashed before my eyes. I didn't know what to say to him or what to do. I just stared. He was right. I began to see even more clearly what my actions had done to him and to our entire family. I remember apologizing repeatedly, promising him that from that moment on his only responsibility would be to enjoy his childhood. He fell into my arms and sobbed. We sobbed together. I assured him that we would pull together and work as a team. From that point on, I fought with every ounce of my being to seek God's direction. After my son left my room that night,

I fell on my knees, sobbing in prayer, and was determined to begin the fight.

The next day would prove enlightening. I arose ready to face life with a renewed sense of purpose. I needed the outcome of this day to be different. As I desperately searched for a plan to reestablish order within my family, I decided in my heart to try and trust God, which was against all intellectual reasoning. I felt an odd mix of desperation and pragmatism. Because of my parents' influence, I knew that God existed when I made the decision to accept Him as my personal Savior at the age of ten. However, I was not able to experience the real power of Christ until later in life through reading and studying the Bible. This new relationship taught me how to step out on faith and actively believe in Him for myself, which was something wholly different and extremely frightening. Up until that moment I had depended solely on my talents. For me, faith was a separate entity. In my mind it was impossible for faith and reason to coexist. Here I was, staring painful relationships and circumstances in the face, but somehow going to God to help me through these crises seemed passive. I preferred a practical approach to solving problems. I needed guarantees. But I realized that to move forward meant complete submission and dependence on God. My mind hadn't operated that

THE MIRACLE—A RENEWED SENSE OF PURPOSE

way before, which made the journey even more challenging. The most frightening part of placing full trust in God was my fear of failure. What if trusting Him was right in theory, but wrong in practice? I questioned myself every step of the way.

On one hand, I felt as though I was taking a dangerous risk by openly acknowledging my faith in God's promise for healing. On the other hand, I was at rock bottom and had nowhere to turn. In the end, what did I have to lose? I had no alternative but to trust God. In retrospect, I was afraid, but I desperately wanted my faith to prevail. So I knew that the first step would have to be to surrender control. Everything hung in the balance and this was my last shot. I knew that if this didn't work, I would never be able to live life fully again.

During the quietness of one early spring morning I was moved by a faint desire in my heart that encouraged me. I forced myself out of bed, showered, dressed, and went downstairs to prepare breakfast for my family. That painful conversation with my son was still fresh and I was determined to make good on my promises to him. So, on that day I did something a little out of character. I grabbed a cup of coffee and sat outside on my small patio to enjoy the sunrise. While listening intently to the birds singing before my children arose for breakfast, I felt like I was listening to a glorious morning concert.

I noticed how the birds didn't seem worried. On the contrary, they appeared happy to greet another day. It occurred to me that birds—creatures that have every right to be scared of the unknown—bless us with their cheerful chirping each morning and are simply content to be alive. For a brief moment I began to envy them for their lack of worry and trust. But as I sat quietly and prayed for healing, the weight of the journey ahead began to feel lighter all of a sudden as tears streamed down my cheeks. Then I felt the warmest rays of the sun on my face. Those rays felt like the palms of God. As I continued to meditate, I heard Him whisper my name within my heart and gently say, "Rhonda, trust me. Let go. I will never leave you, nor forsake you."

As I opened my eyes, I experienced the most calming spirit come over me. It's almost too difficult to explain, but on that morning for the first time in a long time, I was encouraged. That experience was the miracle that I had been waiting for. Looking back, that painful journey helped me to learn that the power of humility is a state of mind. Instead of "being" humble, you have to be willing to be transformed by the Spirit of God. You have to choose to be unconditionally obedient to His will. In the beginning, this wasn't something easy for me to comprehend, but while sitting on the patio that morning with my face and hands extended to heaven,

THE MIRACLE—A RENEWED SENSE OF PURPOSE

I willingly decided to trust that Jesus Christ could heal me. I asked Him for mercy and for one more chance to live life fully again. After that conversation with God, I made the decision not to take medical disability, against all logical reasoning at the advice of my doctor. Instead, I trusted God and committed to consistently obey Him and to be willing to wait as long as it would take for a breakthrough. As far as I was concerned, I had nothing to lose and nowhere else to turn. Besides, after hearing Him reassure me and declare that He wouldn't leave my side, I started to believe with confidence that God would honor my request and help me turn things around.

Several months passed and I began to increase my quiet time in prayer and Bible study. For me, that was the only way I could develop long-lasting trust in God. I figured out that my trust issues with God had to do with not really *knowing* Him. How can you trust someone you don't know? I wanted my trust and faith to be more than a superficial feeling, or worse, wishful thinking. I wanted to completely surrender doubt and fully rest on His promises to help me through my trials. Developing that deep trust in God didn't happen overnight. I had to make a concentrated effort to seek Him every day. Instead of dwelling on my daily fears and anxiety as I did before, I consciously began to practice the art of worshipping God in the middle of challenging circumstances and I deliberately reminded myself of God's power and magnitude. I stopped putting a timetable on God and learned the art of patience and grace. Most importantly, I stopped subconsciously comparing my walk of faith to that of my husband's, which hindered my desire to draw closer to God. I had to keep my eyes focused on what was important and not be diverted by my insecurity of not knowing the Bible as well as my husband did. I was not in a competition. It became clear that I couldn't expect for God to heal me unless I did my part, which was to depend on and believe in His power without reservation. That revelation was huge for me as a logical thinker. If I didn't see it or feel it, then how could it be real?

But unexpectedly, one Sunday morning during worship service, I was praying quietly, thanking God for my anticipated recovery. I asked God, once again, for a miracle. I asked Him to deliver me once and for all from the debilitating depression that had robbed me of joy for years. As I sat in my huge church with over two thousand people surrounding me, at that very moment I felt like I was the only one in the sanctuary, privately worshipping with God all alone. Even as the congregation worshipped collectively, I heard total silence as I worshipped. Suddenly, I experienced an indescribable

THE MIRACLE—A RENEWED SENSE OF PURPOSE

peace come over me and it felt familiar. It was the same feeling that I had also experienced on the patio, but this time it was even more magnified. When I opened my eyes, I was amazed. I looked around and wondered if others had felt a similar experience too, but to my amazement, people were still singing worship songs. I realized that I had had another breakthrough, and this time it felt even more intimate. Though I couldn't prove it, I felt strongly that God had answered my prayer. Spiritually, I felt wonderful and euphoric at first, trying to understand it all. God had come to me not once, but twice. But it wasn't long before my shrewd doubt and pesky logic reared its ugly head and reminded me that in the secular world reality trumps faith any day. Normally logic would override my heart, but for the first time in my life, I didn't care about reason or rationality. I believed in the power of Jesus Christ!

Interestingly, for the next year my health improved exponentially and my doctors were puzzled by my consistent progress. The doctors then determined that I now only needed one of the several medications that I had been prescribed. The dosage became so low that after a while I wondered about its effectiveness. I was feeling so much better, I decided not to ask any questions and instead enjoy my rejuvenated health. However, after several months I did finally ask one of my doctors about how my low dosage could be responsible for managing the depression that at one time had required more than three different medications. His response was shocking. He cleared his throat, looked up from his clipboard, and hesitantly said, "It's not the medicine. Your dosage is too low to make any real impact."

I was puzzled by his response and asked him why he had not said anything until now. "You're an unusual case, Rhonda," he said. "I can't explain the turnaround and your quick recovery, so I thought I'd observe you to determine the accuracy of our original diagnosis." He shifted uncomfortably in his seat and said, "I'm also not sure that you're completely out of the woods. It's quite possible you could have a relapse."

He asked me what I had done differently and concluded that I clearly had needed additional reinforcements besides medication. I left my appointment that day with the understanding that I would continue eating healthy, exercising, and limiting my stressors. As I left his office I reflected on the series of events leading up to the final doctor's visit and realized that his prognosis was indeed another miracle. I had received it one year after my second intimate time of worship with the Lord in church on that one Sunday morning. It took a full year, but I now believed I was truly healed. I was reminded of Peter's walk on the water toward Jesus. I

THE MIRACLE—A RENEWED SENSE OF PURPOSE

could relate to Peter and how he initially had enough faith to get out of the boat, place his feet on the water, and walk toward Jesus. But when his doubts surfaced and he allowed his thoughts to drift to the surrounding storm, he began to sink until Jesus reached for and rescued Him. That is exactly what Jesus did for me. Like Peter, Jesus rescued me as I wavered on the sea of my own doubts. He brought me to Him and truly delivered me from my depression. I couldn't believe the magnitude of Jesus's love to patiently wait with open arms until I was ready to receive His blessing. I sat in my car after my doctor's appointment and smiled as I remembered what God had whispered in my heart on that early spring morning as I listened to the birds. *I will never fail you nor forsake you* (Joshua 1:5). The clouds in my life dissipated and my gray skies were now blue again!

POWER Reflections:

- Develop an exercise and nutritional program to relieve stress. You know your mental and emotional triggers better than anyone.

- Trust God both actively and passively. Learn to not lean on your own strength and understanding. Focus on God and set a time for daily devotional and prayer. The length of time with God is not as important as making a consistent commitment to schedule time with Him.

- When you experience failures throughout life's journey, have joy, get back up, and start again. Learn how to ask God for forgiveness first and forgive yourself second. Failure leads to humility and forgiveness, which are both critical for your Christian walk. Difficult times are when God does His best work because He has your undivided attention.

- Stay in your lane. Do what God has called you to do and own your purpose with the

THE MIRACLE—A RENEWED SENSE OF PURPOSE

gifts that He has bestowed upon you. Do not attempt to do more or less than what God has directed you to do.

- Learn and appreciate the art of being transparent. When you walk in truth and a sense of genuineness, you experience freedom and peace of mind without drowning in fear and anxiety. We are only human. We have to be fair to ourselves and set realistic expectations to be truly successful.

CHAPTER 2:

A New Perspective on Career

"When people go to work, they shouldn't have to leave their hearts at home."

—Betty Bender

"I will instruct you and teach you in the way which you should go: I will counsel you with My eye upon you."

—Psalm 32:8

I truly believe that building a successful career is an outstanding accomplishment. How you think about your career and the value you place on it will drive your other priorities. However, for a long time I viewed success and my career as one in the same. I sometimes still wonder how for so many years I thought chasing my career was a higher priority than my marriage, raising my children, and being true to my faith. As I ponder this question, I think I know when the shift happened. It began when I decided to go into business for myself. When I started my training and consulting business, I concentrated on how I could use my talents to bring in extra income for my family as a stay-at-home mom. My husband and I understood that if I stayed home with the children, it would be a major financial sacrifice, but well worth it.

Initially, when I started my business, I attributed my earliest success to my faith and inspiration from God. However, as my business became more successful, things started to change. I was getting an average of four hours of sleep at night, trying to meet deadlines with limited help. I overcommitted myself on a regular basis as I became more proficient in sourcing business, building teams, and closing contracts more quickly than in the ability to manage high-level long-term projects. Trying to meet the family, personal, and business commitments was overwhelming. While I was building the business, my husband remained employed in a full-time job in aviation and could not have the same flexibility to support me when needed. Even though I understood, it put a little strain on my ability to depend on and trust his full commitment and help in making

A NEW PERSPECTIVE ON CAREER

decisions. Because I was internalizing the stress, I felt as though he was not as invested and committed, which, of course, was not true. I didn't have the luxury of leaving my job as he did at the end of the day because my job was based out of our home. Even when I moved my business out and secured an office downtown, the hours I spent there offered a new set of problems, which impacted the quality of time I spent with my family. My business cycle happened in waves, which in the beginning provided opportunities to rest. But soon with increased marketing and exposure in the business community, I was exposed to an impressive network of high-level senior executives and mentoring groups who targeted me for major business and volunteer opportunities to help grow my business.

Opportunities for growth and exposure were coming from every angle. To capitalize on half of the opportunities presented, I realized that I needed to restructure my business with additional support. Even though I felt these opportunities were well worth my personal sacrifice, I didn't realize the sacrifices my family made along with me. Excitement, pride, and determination superseded my judgment, and I convinced my husband I could do the insurmountable with my wonderful plan of balancing both worlds. I was afraid that I would not get this type of opportunity again and definitely did not want to experience a "Sarah" moment of waiting years for God to answer my prayer of starting my business again only to find myself too old and tired to enjoy it. As business and travel increased, so did additional personal problems in our family life relating to the availability of dependable child care, scheduling conflicts, management of household obligations, and communication breakdowns. Michael and I both worked well together and rarely had any conflict in helping each other, but we usually had the luxury of leaning into our strengths when doing it.

Now I was thrown into managing more on my plate at home and work than I thought was fair, and I harbored much resentment. The business was not really taking into account the needs of my husband or the children, which I was slowly discounting without meaning to. The options for child care and after-school programs were cost restrictive, leaving not much opportunity for family vacations as we had planned. Since I could not change the external factors that were causing stress, I would put my energy into changing my circumstances for the better. I thought if I could increase sales and generate more business to earn more money, then I would have more disposable income to hire people to help me, and that, in essence, would solve my problem. If my strategy worked, then I could hold up my end of

A NEW PERSPECTIVE ON CAREER

the bargain and make good on my promise to Michael. But my plan did not work out as well as I'd hoped, and the cycle of internal pressure and stress continued. The harder I worked in the business, the more I found myself preferring to spend the additional hours trying to create more business and make more money to offer security and peace of mind. I once received immediate gratification and value from building the business; now I was trying to salvage my reputation and a lifestyle that I created based on a false image. I sometimes thought that my peers understood me and my passion for the business better than my family. My entire perspective and reasoning had changed and I did not see it happening. I had lost my overall sense of purpose as it related to how my faith, home, and career fit together because the conflicts were definitely contradicting each other. I did not want to overthink the problem or the solution, but just get through this tough patch and to the next level. I realigned my business and family priorities. For me this translated into prioritizing business values as a core element of my success and moving Christian values down to a lesser but important component. It became more important to validate my self-worth as a businesswoman than to be a fulfilled wife and mother. I struggled with understanding how to merge the two. I felt I had to choose and so did. *I chose my career.* I justified choosing my career by telling myself that the more I gave to my business, the more I was providing for my family. And wasn't lack of time for my husband and children a necessary sacrifice anyway? I started looking at the people around me who had the "success" I thought I wanted and measured their opinions more highly than those of my husband. I wasn't depending on the foundation that had helped me reach my initial success—biblical guiding principles. So naturally, my metrics for success moved toward equating my self-worth with salary, profit, bonuses, and perks. As I brought in more money, my business value went up. It got even tougher when I tried to use those same metrics (financial rewards and material benefits) to measure my role as a Christian wife and mother. While I strongly believed in Christian values, I didn't know how to give 100 percent commitment to all three roles as a wife, mother, and businesswoman without jeopardizing one or all of them. Throughout this time in my life, I believed that I controlled success as long as I positioned myself to meet the right people and created my own opportunities to increase my wealth. But the more energy I placed in designing my idea of success, the more disconnected I became from my family. I was being pulled in two different directions—whether to go to school functions for my children or attend social

A NEW PERSPECTIVE ON CAREER

business functions to meet key contacts. It wasn't long before I unknowingly began rating my successful career as more important than my faith, too.

Now, looking back, I wish I had paid more attention to senior executives and how they prioritized their family values. At the time, all I had heard was that I needed to make sacrifices to impact profitability and that my overachieving would be rewarded with perks and benefits. Today, I know that what I heard wasn't completely true, but I've learned that professionals quickly learn how to position themselves for career advancement, which often means conforming to the cultural mainstream of our organizations. Many of us tend to place our family priorities on the backburner while we're at work. We often don't see this as compromising—putting work before our family and faith is a means to an end. For me, these compromises were fueled by ambition. Learning to balance my ambition with Christian values at work and at home became my missing puzzle piece. I noticed that other professionals like me were struggling with the same thing. Many of us were searching for ways to bring Christ into our careers, not recognizing that it works the other way around. Christ is first and we should design our careers around Him.

For many years, I'd bought into the "bad boy" business image. I enjoyed paying to play. Get what you want just by sheer influence, and if all else fails, intimidation with a smile never hurt. Never did I put much credence into maintaining a Christ-centered approach to career and business, because I knew that the business culture would never support it in a million years. Society doesn't make this easy by recognizing any CEO or business for their Christian principles, even though without them most often they would not be successful in business. In the corporate world, we're admired most for our financial wealth, our intellect, and our influence—all ego-based accolades. We're rarely acknowledged for being good parents in addition to being outstanding at our jobs. Putting faith and family first isn't sexy in the business world or as highly valued as being "successful." As business leaders we have not been convincing enough in illustrating how being happy at home and in our faith impacts our success at work. Instead, we concentrate on the endgame—promotions, raises, and rewards—and leave the process for how to holistically achieve success to our fragile imaginations.

Every self-help book that I'd read over the years said to take control of my own destiny, take charge of my desired outcomes, and own my success and future. Those books provided nuggets of truth, but I still struggled with how to effectively integrate those self-centered principles into my daily life. Then I reached a point when I had to be honest with myself and answer tough questions. How prepared was I to jeopardize my career ambitions and put my home life first? What would that look like?

After I asked these questions, my entire paradigm for both personal and professional success shifted. I found myself no longer able to view Christ from an impersonal perspective, nor could I respond to people in the same manner as I had before. Before I might have been less willing to actually pray about injustices at work or to respectfully voice my concern. I began to challenge myself to view and exercise my faith in Christ differently. On one hand I was so happy that God chose to heal me, but I also knew that healing came with a price. I could no longer take a passive role in sharing why I believed in Christ. Being sensitive to others' views no longer overshadowed my personal relationship and purpose with Christ—a big step for me. Ironically, I believe that my peers saw the change forming in me before I even could acknowledge it myself. I became less arrogant and started having more compassion for my employees, stopped indulging in the need to follow the crowd and attend every happy hour while on the road, and developed other interests. Even though I had worked tirelessly to earn a great reputation in leadership, I wanted to be recognized as a great Christian leader not by title or gender but rather by my character. I wanted to have the right to define who I was as a Christian businesswoman rather than be defined by worldly standards. I was tired of chasing an ideal that I could no longer reach or wanted. It was so funny, because normally I was all about the money, status, and getting more of it, but something inside of me just couldn't do it anymore. In fact, now I viewed my professional accomplishments as a result of obedience to Christ rather than as a symbol of my own greatness. My success went from being all about me to becoming a symbol of God's grace. My success was still my success, but was bestowed upon me as a result of my relationship with Christ. I also gained a better understanding of the value and balance of my roles as a wife, mother, and businesswoman. I came to realize that God is the one who has total control of my life at home, on my job, in my marriage, and in raising my children. I changed the order of my priorities and applied God's wisdom in all situations because I realized that was my only path to success. If you think about it, to be healthy you have to change your lifestyle. It's the same in your spiritual walk. To adopt a healthy godly lifestyle, you have to learn to make positive life choices from God's perspective. You do this by understanding how to apply God's

A NEW PERSPECTIVE ON CAREER

teachings every day. I had to practice daily in order for God's guiding principles to stick! I began to understand the correlation between having faith and believing in God, and how you need both to make wise and positive life choices. My answer became to believe in God, have faith that he would guide me to the outcomes I desired at home and at work, and that I had to make Him part of my everyday routines. I had to relinquish my need for control as I developed a trusting relationship with Him. Until I mastered submission I could not graduate to having balance and harmony with my husband, children, and within my career. I had to believe that God truly did know me before He formed me in my mother's womb and that He specifically designed my talents, skills, and abilities with a burning desire for achievement. I experienced a complete metamorphosis after I submitted to Christ. But at the time I still didn't realize the multitude of generational blessings this would mean for my family and me.

POWER Reflections:

- Seek God for your calling and purpose in your career, family, and marriage. When He provides the vision, accept it and don't run away. Try not to hover in your comfort zone. Be willing to step out and trust what His perfect will for your life will be.

- Be truly humble in your Spirit through giving. It's easy to pretend to dress yourself in a cloak of humility as part of your image. True humility comes from experiencing the Holy Spirit in our lives.

- To whom much is given, much is required. When God delivers you from your painful cross, it is for His purpose and ultimately His glory. Refrain from hiding your blessings under a rock and not sharing them as God has directed you. Your journey was especially designed for the benefit of others, just as Christ's journey was especially designed for us.

- Do not define yourself by your career, income, social status, or possessions.

A NEW PERSPECTIVE ON CAREER

Instead, use your spiritual barometer as a gauge for indication of your true health.

- Wealth is a means to an end, not the end. If God has ordained you to be wealthy, it is for a purpose that is bigger than what you may think. Refrain from trying to design your wealth management program based on today's proven economic strategies. Instead, pray and seek God's divine wisdom to help you reach your full potential. Do not limit yourself. Allow God to lead.

CHAPTER 3:

A New Mentor

"The difference between what we do and what we are capable of doing would suffice to solve most of the world's problems."

—MAHATMA GANDHI

"The beginning of wisdom is: Acquire wisdom: And with all your acquiring get understanding."

—PROVERBS 4:7

In life and especially in business one of the first suggestions offered to up-and-coming executives is to develop a strong network of peers and mentors. We're advised that this group should include successful people that mirror who we are aspiring to become. Most of us begin the quest for a qualified and suitable mentor to rely on for support and guidance. However, many of us seek mentors to propel us to our desired destinations quicker. Even though I see the value in mentorship, I believe Christian professionals should start with the end in mind and seek God's guidance and direction through prayer and meditation before reaching out to find mentors in their careers. I've learned that God guides me through the Holy Spirit—a premise that I found should be used when seeking counsel, especially as it relates to decisions about your future. I now ask God to provide me with tailor-made, Divinely appointed mentors who have the wisdom that I need to navigate various situations in life that have been especially designed by God for my spiritual growth. These mentors can come in multiple shapes and in various forms. Professionals that we are, we tend to love to say that we were mentored and counseled by the best and the brightest—and there's nothing wrong with this. But most often the ones who make the most impact in our lives have poured into our lives at the right times. Think about it: Who are we really listening to as we make daily—and sometimes small—life decisions that eventually turn into critical crossroads? I challenge you to take a closer look at your network, because I believe some of the most encouraging influencers in your life are the least recognized

A NEW MENTOR

people in your network, such as your children, spouse, neighbors, teachers, family friends, grandparents, Bible study leaders, housekeeper, gardener, and parents. We are so busy planning life, we often forget to live it. We sometimes rely solely on logic as we reason our way out of our blessings. God clearly indicates in Proverbs 16:9, "The mind of man plans his way, but the Lord directs his steps." This verse fascinates and frustrates me at the same time because of how we are supposed to apply it in our lives, especially as it impacts our careers. I didn't fully understand the entire meaning of the scripture nor care for my perception of it. My misperception led me to believe that God did not trust my ability to think and plan for myself.

I reasoned that God gave me my career, my talents, and my reputation. I argued that He gave me the ability to reason and think for myself, and that He wouldn't keep His plans a secret. Why would he want me to go about my merry way planning my life rather than saving me time and frustration by just directing me in the first place? I finally learned the answer. Jesus wants to see our heart while we're planning, not just the result of our plans. He wants to see if and how we seek His face for direction as we plan, and if we really value Him as our Lord and Savior in all that we do. He wants to see if our heart for Christ is genuine and measures up to the motives and expected outcomes of our plans. Once I learned that, I began to reevaluate my motives for why I wanted to excel in my career and why I needed the promotions. I began to wonder if my desires were aligned with God's direction or if I was feeding my ego. Sometimes as our careers excel, our motivations become blurred in the process. The climb to the "top" is rife with competitiveness, fear, greed, and satisfying others' needs, and we tend to forget why we actually were attracted to our careers in the first place.

If we seek His voice and are trained to recognize it within us, we prepare ourselves to make the tough calls even when they go against the mainstream. This was an epiphany for me as I came across the scripture in Psalm 25:12–14, "Who is the man who fears the Lord? He will instruct him in the way he should choose, his soul will abide in prosperity, and his descendants will inherit the land. The secret of the Lord is for those who fear Him. And He will make them know His covenant." I interpreted this scripture to mean that it is more important for me to be in awe of God by fearing His power and deity over my life and respecting His ability to lead me than for me to do it on my own, whether it appeared logical or not.

I experienced this painful lesson many years ago right before I closed my business. Upon returning from

A NEW MENTOR

an unsuccessful business trip in Seattle, Washington, my business associate and I had argued over severing our current business relationship. Over several months leading up to this heated discussion, God had been quietly showing me that it was time for us to split up. However, I couldn't bring myself to make the decision. I wanted to continue our path even though we were not seeing eye to eye. I was trying to work through it. I thought that my sheer determination was enough. I was wrong, and during my last trip with him in Seattle we both decided after a very heated discussion that we would sever the relationship permanently. But once again, his words resonated with me for years after we departed, and I remember one phrase that rang in my head as I was closing my business shortly thereafter. He said, "Rhonda, you'll never be successful in business because you don't know how to put your faith first, business second, and family third!" His words were disappointing and contradicted how I perceived my faith. I already felt guilty at that time for mixing faith and business together, but the stress of juggling family and career had taken its toll and I had nowhere else to turn in my mind. Based on my knowledge of the Bible, I believed that God did not want us to prioritize our family behind our jobs. But when I worked in the corporate and business environments, the culture was anything but nurturing, to say the least, and indirectly forced us to prioritize family in that manner. I was confused. If God created all mankind, and we are all created in His image, and all of us are designed for a purpose, then our focus must be realigned to mirror our new identity. There were times I did not know who I should represent. Should I be a Christian, a woman, a black woman, a businesswoman, a mother, or a wife first? Unless we take the time to research our ideals and standards for living, we will allow others' doubts and ideals to overshadow what we know to be true. Our career should be an extension of who we are as the person that God created us to be.

Sometimes I wonder why I am not overly impressed with the rich and famous. I look at them through a different set of lenses. Instead of seeking pictures and autographs, I tend to think about them as people with real lives, real problems, and real needs. I wonder if their faith has sustained them. I try to see people from God's perspective as stated in Psalm 139:14, "for I am fearfully and wonderfully made."

Our mentors and circle of influence should help propel us in accentuating the natural and spiritual person that God has created us to be. I can't bring myself to wish to be anyone else other than myself. The positive outcome of this trait is that you can lead and influence

A NEW MENTOR

people to make positive changes within their lives; the negative is that you open up yourself to allowing people to want to emulate you in some form or fashion. We all tend to need others to validate our worth, and we should be careful of seeking mentors as a way of doing it. I remember as a child complaining profusely to my mother about several of my childhood girlfriends who were imitating some of my ideas and traits at school. It would infuriate me and I would run to her for solace and advice to put them straight. I waited patiently for Mom to come up with a brilliant idea. Instead, mom would look at me with one of her teacher expressions and say, "Rhonda, chin up, girl. Imitation is the best form of flattery! Now go out and flatter the world!" I would run out of her presence with such zeal and excitement, thinking I was doing something great. Later I realized that she really did not give me any solution to my problem. Now I get it. Mom was trying to tell me to be myself and not worry about how others perceived me. I've also learned not to put anyone on a pedestal higher than God because no man is better or worse than the next. Mom would remind me and say, "No matter how famous people are or think they are, they put on their pants one leg at a time, just like you and me." She was right, and this shaped me over the years. Her advice helps me keep life in perspective. Even though I appreciate the magnitude of hard work that notable people accomplish to attain significant milestones in their life, I tend to think about them as people becoming more interested in their true motivators for stepping out on faith fueling their achievements. One such person was Martin Luther King. To this day, I rarely hear people talk about why he must have been so dedicated to the Lord in order to make the sacrifices that he did, or how he developed a faith so strong that he moved a nation as he did. How did he receive the Holy Spirit? Was he superhuman, or just like you and me? Were there times when he was scared and could trust no one but God, regardless of the accomplishment and fame? Though King was a remarkable man, as a leader, I've reminded myself that his leadership was steeped in faith, a relationship with God, and putting God's purpose for his life before his own fears, desires, and ambitions.

Over the years, people have asked me who my role models are in life. As you seek mentors, instead of assuming that the image of the person you admire is perfect, I encourage others to ask clarifying questions. Don't be afraid to question if their approach to life aligns with yours. There is one phenomenal woman I reference as the mother of all mentors, and she is the woman referenced in Proverbs 31:10–31. Here's what the scripture says:

A NEW MENTOR

A wife of noble character who can find? She is worth far more than rubies. Her husband has full confidence in her and lacks nothing of value. She brings him good, not harm, all the days of her life. She selects wool and flax and works with eager hands.

She is like the merchant ships, bringing her food from afar.

She gets up while it is still night; she provides food for her family and portions for her female servants. She considers a field and buys it; out of her earnings she plants a vineyard. She sets about her work vigorously; her arms are strong for her tasks. She sees that her trading is profitable, and her lamp does not go out at night.

In her hand she holds the distaff and grasps the spindle with her fingers. She opens her arms to the poor and extends her hands to the needy. When it snows, she has no fear for her household; for all of them are clothed in scarlet. She makes coverings for her bed; she is clothed in fine linen and purple. Her husband is respected at the city gate, where he takes his seat among the elders of the land. She makes linen garments and sells them, and supplies the merchants with sashes. She is clothed with strength and dignity;

*she can laugh at the days to come. She speaks
with wisdom, and faithful instruction is on
her tongue. She watches over the affairs of her
household and does not eat the bread of idleness.
Her children arise and call her blessed; her
husband also, and he praises her:*

*"Many women do noble things, but you
surpass them all."*

*Charm is deceptive, and beauty is fleeting;
but a woman who fears the Lord is to be praised.*

*Honor her for all that her hands have done,
and let her works bring her praise at the city gate.*

I experienced my metamorphosis and it was important that I find someone I could identify with, someone who could provide sound guidance and encouragement at the height of feeling lost in my career. As I began searching, it was apparent that trying to find one person who had mastered marriage, parenting, and career successfully while also being a Christian would be challenging. As I searched for the right mentor, I wondered yet again if I was trying to accomplish the impossible. I wondered if I should instead look for multiple mentors as guides rather than expecting to identify one particular person who had mastered all the areas I was seeking to master, too.

A NEW MENTOR

Successful women tend to be multifaceted and multilayered with various complexities. Yes, I know that I am a woman, but I have always viewed myself as much more than that. I am a leader, an influencer, and a motivator for change. I thoroughly enjoy motivating people to accomplish greatness within their lives and circle of influence. It is so rewarding for me to meet women and men of all walks of life who have walked the walk and talked the talk with excellence, exhibiting their confidence, but with a humble spirit. As a successful professional, I am sure you have been approached by several professionals wanting you to become their mentor. When someone approaches me with the request of becoming a mentor, before I respond, I usually ask him or her specifically to tell me why he or she chose me. Usually, but not always, I find that their request was prompted by the professional image that I project. However, I would debate with anyone that the real attribute that draws people to me is not my image, as they might think, but Christ within me. My actions and reactions to life, including my choices, beliefs in fairness, handling disappointment, trusting others, respecting others, and my work ethic, are all spiritually oriented virtues.

These virtues I found and modeled from my mentor—the woman in Proverbs 31. I realized that she was the epitome of who I needed to guide me in my journey. Admittedly, in the beginning, I admired her for all the wrong reasons. I was looking for the proverbial shortcut—a list of qualities that could dictate my actions without having to dig deep. The Proverbs 31 woman truly had it all and, according to the scriptures, excelled in everything that she did. She first and foremost loved and feared the Lord and respected her family. She was married to a hardworking, financially stable man who was well respected in the community, and had children who adored her and made both her and her husband proud. She was an accomplished businesswoman and role model and was well known in social circles for her humble spirit and generosity. She was cultured and appreciated the fine qualities of life and what they afforded her as demonstrated in her fashionable wardrobe and home furnishings. She also helped promote her husband whenever possible by working with him and, through it all, she had a smile and humble spirit.

I have been fortunate in my career to partner with businesswomen who have been strong family women as well. We had many discussions about our preconceived notions of the purpose of career, family, and marriage before we had developed a serious relationship with Christ. As a child I was constantly challenged to excel

A NEW MENTOR

and do my best with continual reminders that girls were as competitive as boys. This sparked my desire for competition and recognition, which later challenged my thoughts about the benefits of marriage and children. I believed that by having a successful career I could separate myself from the pack. I wanted to be recognized for a significant accomplishment, and at that time I viewed motherhood as mundane. I thought that any woman could have a child, but not anyone could achieve a notable successful career. I desired to be defined as a leader, a mover and shaker, and achieve success by my standards, my way. This may seem sexist, but I never wanted to emulate women but rather men, in particular powerful businessmen. I noticed that it was easier for me to identify with businessmen because men had the know-how and opportunity to create wealth. They also appeared to enjoy the influence and power that came with it. Men have always enjoyed competition and the thrill of it. The men I most admired enjoyed the competition more than "winning" the prize. In my career, I believed men had the freedom to be themselves, which then elevated their self-confidence and validation tenfold. Because I was wired competitively, I could easily relate to that. I was always taught that I could do anything if I put my mind to it. However, it appeared that between society, biblical doctrine, and cultural influences, the value placed on women was hidden under several layers of preconceived limitations. This observation was far more evident with the struggles women raising children experience.

The image of a successful dad was vastly different from that of a successful mom. Men simply were not challenged or viewed in the same fashion as women. In my experience, fathers appeared to live life to the fullest regardless of their circumstances, whereas mothers had to endure the brunt of child rearing with limited support. Traditionally, the most important characteristic respected in men was not their parenting skills but rather their business acumen and ability to provide financially for their families. So you can see why I was in a quandary wanting to play in a male arena to experience the freedom and benefits, all the while trying to emulate my Proverbs 31 role model of femininity and grace. My aspirations consumed me and fueled the fire. My milestones were derived from my definition of success. I believed that I was effectively translating the Proverbs 31 achievements relative to those of my generation. Thus, I quickly developed a "to do" list of goals relative to the Proverbs 31 achievements. As I share them with you, I challenge you to determine which ones really bring peace of mind. My list looked something like this: I am a Christian, check;

A NEW MENTOR

I have obtained advanced degrees, check; I attended a reputable school, check; I am happily married *or so I thought*, check; I have children, check; my children attend private schools, check; I have a beautiful home in a nice neighborhood, check; we have nice cars, check; I have a purebred dog, check; I have a small but tailored wardrobe, check; I have a handsome husband with a great career, check; I know how to dress to impress, check; I have people who admire me, check; I am an accomplished professional with awards, check; I am a business owner, check; I have earned six-figure salaries, check; I know influential people, check; I work in the community, check. I was on the road to having it all—or so I thought.

POWER Reflections:

- Discern when to ask for God's help and when He is directing you to ask for help from your family and others. Asking God for help when you are truly in need is a sign of spiritual maturity. Even though it may feel like weakness, asking God for help instead of solving problems without His direction actually shows your strength.

- Being right isn't always right. Sometimes being silent and praying in the Spirit allows the Lord to direct your words, tone, and body language. Silence often speaks volumes and better accomplishes our goals. Pray and be deliberate when speaking.

- Learn the art of encouragement and give freely to others daily, especially to your family members. Instead of practicing the art of "doing" for others all of the time, practice the art of helping others "do for themselves" by encouraging them to apply their gifts given to them from the Lord—especially as it relates to your children.

CHAPTER 4:

A Newfound Respect for My Husband

"Great minds have great purposes, others have wishes. Little minds are tamed and subdued by misfortune; but great minds rise above them."

—Washington Irving

"Her husband is known in the gates, when he sits among the elders of the land."

—Proverbs 31:23

The word "respect" has a different meaning depending on whom you ask. Some people view respect as a willingness to do what is asked of you without question; some as a prize earned through career accomplishments or status. Before my transformation, I thought respect was synonymous with wealth, influence, and power. I know now that influential leaders are respected not by the material possessions that they own, but by how they treated others along the way as they grew in their career success. I used to only respect the leaders who lived up to my wealth and status standards. At work, I weighed my level of respect for others by their title, function, and level of responsibility. More responsibility, which often coincided with higher salaries, was a key factor in determining whether I respected someone or not. The idea of status over substance eventually bled over into my personal life and caused a breakdown in our family's harmony. I went to my husband one day and asked what he thought about my perception and definition of respect. Did he think that I was accurate in thinking power came through having influence and material possessions, or should I re-evaluate what respect meant to me? His response surprised me.

"Rhonda," he said, "I don't doubt that you love me as your husband, but we've never been able to talk about what respect means to both of us."

Looking back on it, Michael was right. We had been married for over thirty years and never took the time to stop and ask the burning question of what respect means to each of us. We knew that it was important,

A NEWFOUND RESPECT FOR MY HUSBAND

but we didn't know exactly how we should demonstrate those lessons to each other and our children. I thought the best way to structure my family's hierarchy was to design it like a small corporation. Michael was the CEO, I was vice president, and our children were junior executives in training. This idea did not go well. Instead of looking to God and asking Him what roles each family member should execute, I tried to force my family into my misguided idea of what respect should entail. I had preconceived notions and wanted my husband to make more money than me because he was the CEO. I didn't realize at the time that money didn't equal power.

I also felt that my husband should be well practiced in budgeting, forecasting, and leadership, and successful in business operations in managing our home. I believed this was what it meant to be a CEO. Most importantly, I expected our family to reflect his outstanding leadership. I became committed to having our family look a certain way—order, discipline, and growth were my pillars for ensuring our family was on the right track. After I designed our family structure around these principles, it was obvious to me what God wanted and needed my help to do. I needed to transform Michael into the leader he needed to be as our family's CEO. If my husband transformed, I would finally feel more comfortable following his lead . . . or so I thought. This journey for the next nine years was a total disaster and a waste of my time and energy. My marriage, family, and career became exhausting and I lost perspective of what was important. I thought I was on the right track and didn't understand where I lost perspective. Instead of designing my family life within a corporate leadership model, I should have worked with my husband and children to design our own special model based on who we are as individuals, with God at the center guiding our every move. My heart was in the right place, but that was yet another instance where I had to control the outcome instead of allowing God to lead the way.

The turning point in my marriage happened right as I struggled to overcome my depression. I looked around one day and noticed none of my most trusted business colleagues and supporters were present as I was desperately battling unhappiness. The only person by my side was my husband. Even though my husband had always been an intellectual, quiet, and reserved man, for some reason I expected him to also fit into my idea of what a "successful" man should be. Unfortunately, most of my images of successful men were generated from media. I wanted a wealthy man who also took responsibility for my happiness. My favorite show growing up was *The Brady Bunch*. I ran around the house singing their theme song a thousand times a day. I enjoyed the family interaction and story lines. I shared with my sister my dreams of one day growing up and meeting a man just like Mike Brady to marry, but with fewer kids, of course. One day in a moment of fury, my sister loudly screamed at me that *The Brady Bunch* was a stupid TV show and that life for black people could never be that way. According to her, I was "silly" for dreaming I would have a *Brady Bunch* life one day. After that outburst and reality check, I went looking for another model for my family to follow with similar standards. Years later, I found solace in *The Cosby Show*. Not only did we share the same ethnicity and culture, but they also showed an ideal balance between money and the importance of personal relationships within the family.

I realized then how selfish I had become in putting the weight of being the CEO of our family on my husband. I could never have lived up to the financial expectations I placed on him. My husband's strengths had nothing to do with his salary. His greatest strength was his passion and commitment to the Lord, but I mistook his humility and dedication to family as a weakness. He would always put our personal life before his professional life. Since he didn't have the status I expected of him, I never realized how positive his impact was on our family. Our children needed more than growing up with stable finances to become successful, happy adults. Our adult sons still call him often to ask questions. They share details about their families and adventures in the business world, all while gaining insight and encouragement from their father. It's so gratifying to hear the laughter, pride, and love in their voices. Moments like those make me grateful that Michael and I were able to hang in there during those difficult years.

In the depths of my depression, I thought God was punishing me for my lofty career aspirations. I began thinking about the comments made to me by others in the past. Was I trying to prove them wrong? Was I too ambitious? Did I want too much? Was I too driven? At times, I thought that I wasn't smart enough or grateful enough. The thought had even crossed my mind that I had married the wrong man and had children too soon. The self-doubt continued, until one day during my healing and transformation I realized it had nothing to do with any of those reasons. It all had to do with my lack of trust in God to lead my life. The bottom line was that I was afraid that God would not give me the desires of my heart in the way that I had envisioned. I was so consumed with fear and doubt that I had convinced myself that the only way to succeed was to influence the process. Excessive reasoning was my downfall. I relied on my flawed logic, education, and research to rein-

A NEWFOUND RESPECT FOR MY HUSBAND

force my perceived power rather than the true power of Christ in my life. To have the happiness and joy in my marriage that I craved, I'd have to refocus and trust that God would change my perspective about my husband. I needed God to teach me how to respect him as he rightfully deserved. I would now have to evolve from the mover-and-shaker businesswoman that I had tirelessly developed over the years to a patient, loving, and respectful wife willing to make the tough sacrifices that my marriage urgently needed.

Adopting that mindset was hard for me because I had to reframe the way I thought about marriage, my husband, and respect overall. I began treating my husband differently.

I struggled with how to restructure my marriage, knowing that I had tried a business model in the past, and that approach had failed. In deep prayer with the Lord about how I wanted to become a better wife, I heard Him say, "Rhonda, it's okay to see your husband as your family's CEO. But from now on, see your husband as a CEO I designed especially for your family. View him through My eyes. In him, I've created a leader, father, and husband who deserves the love, grace, and mercy of a faithful partner. Stop seeing him as an infallible superior. He's not perfect and neither are you."

In the morning, I practiced greeting him with a

smile. I made a point to be supportive of his decisions, become more encouraging, change my authoritative tone in our conversations, and make an effort to respect his downtime. We began to schedule appointed times to talk and vent issues that were important to both of us, such as purchasing a new home, vacationing abroad, taking up new hobbies for both of us, hiring a personal trainer, and getting back involved with community projects that we firmly supported. We also listened and communicated more with one another. We set realistic boundaries for our relationship and for raising our children. I also asked him to share his dreams and goals for himself and our family—much like a CEO would share his vision about the company's direction and goals for the year. As a CEO would ensure that he involved his entire executive team in helping to create his vision, I wanted to show my love and support by working with Michael as a true partner in designing a family model that works for the entire Gaines household. I yearned to hear and see that glimmer of confidence in his eye again, knowing that I believed in him and would once again be his biggest champion. You can tell a lot about a man in the way he thinks. But you can tell so much more about him in the way he dreams and plans for his future. I asked him what he needed to accomplish his goals and as I shared my goals with him, we explored

A NEWFOUND RESPECT FOR MY HUSBAND

together how we could use our God-given skills, talents, and abilities to help support our renewed family vision. We began to pray more consistently together, both in the morning before he went to work and at night before we went to bed. I made a point to have dinner ready for the family five nights a week and even held dinner for him as a symbol of my respect for him if I knew he'd be home late. For me, cooking dinner for my family was symbolic of how committed I was in a way I hadn't been before.

I also showed my love in other more subtle ways. In the mornings, I intentionally prepared a cup of coffee for him before he went to work. One fall morning as the weather started to become cooler, I awoke early and prepared his favorite breakfast with freshly ground coffee. I placed it on a beautifully decorated serving tray on his nightstand as he was taking his shower before he left for work, something I would never have done in the past. But this particular morning I wanted to do something special for him. He came back into the bedroom, saw the breakfast feast, and looked at me with a puzzling smirk. "Is everything okay?" he asked. "Yes. In fact, everything is perfect. I thought you would enjoy a good breakfast this morning because you had mentioned to me last night that your schedule would be quite challenging today. Mike, I wanted to encourage you and to let you know how much I love you," I said and handed him a personal card of encouragement from me. He looked at me with warmth and appreciation in his eyes and said, "Thank you, love. Rhonda, I love you so much, you know that."

A remarkable shift occurred. The more effort I made, the more effort he made. Our marriage improved and we began to communicate more regularly. With our increased communication, we also learned how to disagree respectfully. We made a promise to each other that we would never go to bed angry. Every argument was ended respectfully, and if we didn't have the time or patience, we would schedule another time to continue our discussion. Instead of pushing my agenda onto my husband when making major decisions, I shared my opinions and recommendations as his trusted advisor, and would listen respectfully to his input. I made a conscious effort to work as a partner in my marriage, and not have divorce be an easy way out. Most importantly, I had to stop comparing him to other men who I thought were better in business and negotiation. It was unfair to compare him to someone I didn't know personally.

For our finances, we both agreed that if something we wanted to buy was not in our budget, then it should not be purchased until we could afford it, rather than living beyond our means.

I have always gravitated toward a more luxurious lifestyle. It became difficult to keep up with that lifestyle when it started to affect the quality of life for my family. My family often became frustrated with me because I was constantly trying to accomplish my next life goal. It was hard for me at first to see my friends buying these things, but I soon learned that we all have different bank accounts, opportunities, and life plans directed for us by God. Even though all of us are created equal, God did not say that all of us would be financially equal in every season of our lives. By allowing yourself to accept your situation, you'll ultimately find more happiness than always chasing after the approval of your peers.

POWER Reflections:

- Refrain from "fixing" your husband as God reveals to you what he lacks in his spiritual growth. Instead, pray and fast for his breakthrough and ask God for peace to wait on Him as he sets his deliverance in motion.

- Learn how to effectively communicate with your husband beyond the bedroom. Prayer is the ultimate form of communication and is longstanding. Pray in the morning together before you both begin your day and at night before you retire for the evening. When traveling, adjust your schedules to connect with each other—even briefly before the end of the day. Remember that your relationship with God sets the tone for both your hearts and brains to collide.

- Your husband is the leader of the home by God's design, which does not limit your value and influence as a wife. Help him lead with the gifts that God has given you, and if you feel uncomfortable in doing so as I originally did, then ask God to show you how to get it done so that you can truly get on board.

- Stop comparing your husband to other men whom you believe exceed your expectations. Our lives are a reflection of trusting God.

CHAPTER 5:

Discovering the True Purpose of Family

"The attitude you have as a parent is what your kids will learn from more than what you tell them. They don't remember what you try to teach them. They remember what you are."

—Jim Henson

"Strength and dignity are her clothing and she smiles at the future. Give her the product of her hands, and her works praise her in the gates."

—Proverbs 31:25, 31

As I went through the many layers of my transformation as a wife, I also experienced similar challenges as a mother raising our children. No matter how much I achieved in my career, the stress of striving to "have it all"—and to keep it all—especially affected how I raised my children. Even with a spouse, being a mother was more challenging than I ever expected. Let me say this: I am so very grateful that I had my three beautiful, loving, and talented children whom I greatly respect and admire. They have given me a newfound appreciation for life and have helped me to grow into the woman I am today. But before I came to this realization, I admit I had not planned on having children. My perception was that children were a lot of work. I saw them as expensive liabilities that immediately began sucking your energy from inside your womb and put excessive demands on your life until you were in the tomb. Imagine my surprise when I found out after we got married that my husband wanted six children—a subject we conveniently forgot to discuss before we said "I do." Thankfully, God had other plans and we happily stopped at three children.

The reason I was hesitant to have children in the first place was because I believed that children hindered your career. Children are expensive and I knew that as a mother I would be forced to make financial sacrifices to provide them with a comfortable lifestyle. Once again, every idea or belief I had about family was driven by my career ambitions. I had no idea how to raise children. I was the youngest of four children without any infant nieces or nephews on which to practice. I grew up mainly around adults and was more adult focused. However, I did appreciate the fact that other couples made it look so easy. Looking back, sometimes it seems as though I held my breath the entire twenty years of raising our children because I was so afraid that I would mess up somehow and make a mistake that could not be reversed. My anxiety was precipitated by several factors, one being that we began our family when I was twenty-four. Most of our professional friends were not even married, and if they were, they did not start a family until they were in their forties. The friends who did not have the responsibility of children were not as sensitive and understanding as to why we could not leave our three children behind and invest our money in a vacation just for the two of us. Those days were long gone, even though we needed a vacation. Soon our invitations became few and far between because money to pay for a family of five did not come easy.

We also dealt with the private-school culture—a world I had never experienced before. Preparing for your child's education was a daunting task. The costs were similar to college tuition except with private school, parents are also expected to help teach. Growing up, I had always attended public school and was not aware of or prepared for the enormous workload required from our children. I had to learn how to better support them by helping to find additional resources for tutoring and learning. The children's social calendar soon became more demanding than mine. As a mother and wife, I was expected to ensure that everyone's daily schedule was successfully achieved without any mishaps along the way. Another challenge was managing the costs for their tuition against fun activities for our family. Because of the inconsistency of my business income, our vacations were sometimes limited to stay-at-home vacations, which were rarely relaxing for me. At the height of raising our kids, my immediate family lived out of state, and couldn't take the kids off my hands when I needed time to regroup.

Parenting provided a unique set of challenges for my husband and I. I had grown up in the country, so my concept of family was very informal—it wasn't uncommon to have relatives dropping by unannounced all of the time. We would call our home "Grand Central Station." My husband came from a more formal upbringing, so parenting as a cohesive unit required many nights of discussions and compromises. I remember each summer taking the children to Virginia to stay at their grandparents'. My husband, Mike, would lecture the children for forty-five minutes prior to arriving, advising them not to walk barefoot because of the dangerous germs that they could catch. I, of course, tried to explain that I had gone barefoot most of my life and grew up fine, but he had his own opinions. Our children quietly listened and each year as we said our goodbyes and waved to them as we drove away, I would see from my rearview mirror their shoes being thrown high into the air in my parents' front yard.

To this day when I think of the highs and lows in parenting, I don't know how I did it while keeping a positive perspective. I continually experienced anxiety, wondering if I was balancing life effectively and how the children would turn out as adults. No matter how well you think you are doing, there is always that doubt in the back of your mind. So as I had done with my marriage, I knew exactly where to turn when I started to feel anxious for solutions on becoming a better mother—my mentor. Of course I couldn't call the Proverbs 31 woman and take her out to lunch. But I could read about what influenced her to be prosperous and what her guiding life principles were. If she could achieve balance, then I knew I could too. Besides, she was a woman just like me. That realization alone inspired and encouraged me. She and I were in the same boat by being married and balancing family. So I studied Proverbs 31 voraciously to learn how she approached motherhood. All Christian parents should read Proverbs. It offers basic life principles like Proverbs 3:27: "Do not withhold good from those to whom it is due, When it is in your own power to do it." I used this principle to teach my children about the power of giving to others.

Since we didn't have extra money for extra-curricular activities, I consciously decided to give my children the best that I did have—my love, support, and wisdom. I also thought I could put what I had learned throughout my years in business to good use and share those lessons with them. I had the idea to turn our dinner table into the "boardroom" for training our future leaders—our children. I used the "boardroom" symbolism as an opportunity for my husband and me to teach our children how to think as leaders. The Bible provided excellent examples of leadership skills at all levels. We developed rules for the dinner-table discussions, which included dinner attire, timeliness, and manners. Each of the children took turns saying grace and participating in our family discussions. My husband and I would pre-select discussion topics that were related to current events and ask their opinions.

DISCOVERING THE TRUE PURPOSE OF FAMILY

We encouraged them to respectfully discuss and debate their positions. Most importantly, we taught leadership skills and helped them explore how to be a leader in every environment from the classroom to sports settings. It was also important for us to encourage and praise them at the dinner table for their accomplishments. That, paired with explaining how to handle difficult situations and disappointments in work, school, or social settings using biblical teachings and specific ways to apply them, made for enriching conversations between all of us. An important principle of our new boardroom approach to parenting included how we responded to significant awards or recognitions. We encouraged them to credit how their faith in Christ was represented in their achievements. We challenged them to look for signs of Jesus's blessing manifesting in the midst of their trials. We also often prayed for breakthroughs together as a family by asking the children to list their goals and challenges and praying together for guidance and deliverance. In our boardroom, we had big family hugs as often as possible, though sometimes we had to get by with a couple times a week because of our hectic schedules. At the request of our youngest son, we created a blessing jar for our boardroom. Our blessing jar was an empty glass container that we used to collect note cards where we described the prayer requests that God had answered over time. At the end of the year on New Year's Eve, we would read every blessing as a family. Our blessing jar was a wonderful demonstration of how faithful God is to us and taught our children the benefit of exercising our faith daily.

Another blessing for my husband and me was spending quality time with our children by taking them to school each morning. Part of our family time included prayer with them in the car while traveling. We also cooked, learned sewing, and even educated them about finances.

The boardroom helped transform the way we raised our children by building a true foundation for their success. By following God's guidance, I see that we were planting seeds of confidence, self-esteem, and hope through our children that have been watered over the years by so many other wonderful people who have poured wisdom and love into their lives. If it were not for the foundation that we provided, they would not have the success that they have today. This transformation may have started with me, but through my obedience and God's grace it has transferred to my husband and children and to so many others who have crossed our paths. Obedience to the Lord offers such freedom, peace, and blessings.

POWER Reflections:

- Encourage teachable family moments at the dinner table drawn from discussions about life's lessons and how we should allow God to respond to our various circumstances. Praise your children when they share their lessons and daily blessings.

- Plan for vacations—whether formal or a stay-at-home vacation. Make them fun and special for yourself and your family. Pausing your daily routine refreshes you and stimulates your mind.

- Don't leave your spouse behind as you grow in your career. Learn to communicate to God at an increased level the higher you go up within your career. Because with it comes increased responsibility, pressure, and anxiety, leaving room for our marriages to be impacted negatively. Fight for the marriage at all costs by fighting for your souls first in growing close to God. When you grow closer to God then all else has a chance of falling into place.

CHAPTER 6:

Preparing Children to Succeed in Life

"Courage doesn't always roar. Sometimes courage is the quiet voice at the end of the day saying, 'I will try again tomorrow.'"

—Mary Anne Radmacher

"The fear of the Lord is the beginning of knowledge. Fools despise wisdom and instruction."

—Proverbs 1:7

People sometimes think that successful professionals are mathematicians because at the end of the day, it is all about profit, crunching numbers, and making money. In all honesty, being good at math is not the only key to being an effective executive. A good businessperson has to easily transition from thinking inside the box to outside the box with a high level of strategic and tactical maneuvering. Now, I would agree that math helps strengthen strategic prowess. But the ability to succeed in business is really determined by your ability to solve problems and influence people. Successful businesspeople are typically intuitive and know the right questions to ask at the right times to help solve problems quickly—this ultimately increases profit. With that in mind, when I searched for activities for our children, chess caught my attention. Chess was a game that strengthened their ability to think, strategize, and solve problems. We of course encouraged sports, but we loved nudging them toward mentally stimulating and strategic games, too. We found that through our parenting, we could adopt some of the principles I found working for companies. But instead of profit, our faith would be the foundation and success would mean a strengthened and powerful spiritual walk with God.

As my husband and I considered chess, I couldn't help but think of my mother. As a high school math teacher for more than forty years, she made us take every advanced math course offered in high school. I complained, citing that I could never be good at it. Her patient response is what I instill in my own children today. She said, "I am not as concerned about your grades as with how you think and solve problems." After she said that I felt like a weight was lifted. Then she said, "Remember, there's more than one way to solve a math problem, just as there is always more than one way to solve problems in life. That is why you should never give up because there will always be another option!" Tackling those math courses increased my persistence and fortitude. I'm empowered to overcome my circumstances rather than wait for someone else to answer it for me.

My parents also taught me several life lessons that helped us to raise our children. The first lesson was simple: Life is not fair, and to get through it you should understand the value of having faith in Jesus Christ. They approached our faith as a necessity rather than as an option because they did not want us to feel helpless when faced with impossible situations. Our parents knew that we would inevitably experience disappointment. They took the time on several occasions to share how their faith sustained them in insurmountable life circumstances and why it was important to them. They also explained how it would benefit us. They encouraged us to attend church with them regularly and to ask as many questions that came to our minds about our faith.

I was encouraged to participate in youth activities in church and at school. My mom regularly included me in events involving public speaking and presentations to help improve my written and oral communication. I learned the benefit and technique of putting a positive spin on any situation rather than concentrating on the negative circumstances. Instead, I was encouraged to focus on what I could control and pray to God to intervene and do the rest. My parents' consistent encouragement was paramount. No matter what I attempted to do, I knew that my parents were in my corner regardless of the outcome. They viewed failure as a necessary stepping-stone toward achieving success rather than allowing failure to define me as a person. I was so grateful that no matter what challenges I experienced, home was my refuge.

When my children were young and my husband and I had to make decisions about their education and select the schools we wanted them to attend, I asked the advice of my mom. We wanted to know how best to support our children, especially during their early formative years. My husband and I researched so many schools and finally decided to enroll them in private school as long as we could afford to make the financial sacrifice. I was amazed at the amount of homework required by the teachers but held high hopes and expectations for

PREPARING CHILDREN TO SUCCEED IN LIFE

their future. As I was venting to my mother one day about the expenses and homework, she told me that the perspective of educators in the private schools is slightly different than in public schools. In private schools, the child's educational experience is designed as a partnership between the parents, students, and teachers. The classroom experience evaluates if the student is learning at home and if we as parents are involved in their education. So as my husband and I sent our children to private schools, my mother reminded me to schedule enough time for my husband and me to review homework, provide additional educational resources to help our children, and to stay up-to-date with the material they were learning. I took her advice and made the necessary sacrifices for our children, and now am proud to say that I have passed the torch on to my adult children as they are now teaching our grandchildren—an example of the power of generational blessings!

While writing this book I asked my children this question: "What were the most important lessons you learned while growing up?" Their responses melted my heart. According to them, they learned how to carry themselves, how to pray, that they should do what they enjoy, and the importance of dinnertime. In the words of one of my sons:

There are so many aspects of growing up that

revolved around self-development. Items like how to shake a hand, how to eat at a fancy restaurant, what a full place setting looks like, how to walk with confidence, how to dress for an interview, looking others in the eye, understanding consequences of life lessons, and understanding that even if I brought home F's on my report card, you loved me in spite of my less than superior academic achievement. You and dad taught me true responsibility, not the worldly version. You taught me how to own up to my mistakes, as I was told and taught from the beginning that I was a leader. As a leader, I was held to a higher standard from the very beginning, and as such, was expected to live accordingly. I gained much from the many conversations regarding taking initiative, and not waiting for people or opportunities to simply land in my lap. It is this latter lesson that has helped me the most as I move in my early career.

Prayer was a hallmark in our family. No matter what the situation or issue, prayer was always at the center. Additionally, as I grew in my personal faith, I now see that even in our prayer life as a family, prayers were not simply, "Lord, gimme, gimme," but truly following The Lord's Prayer, using the Acknowledgment, Confession, Thanksgiving, and Supplication (A.C.T.S.) approach. This approach in learning how to pray is discussed in biblical teaching to help you acknowledge the deity and power of God rather than seeing Him as a mysterious genie responsible for answering our prayers. Also, it could have been so easy to fall into the trap of false prayer in a "name it—claim it" kind of mentality. Though we did pray with confidence, we did not dictate to the Lord what it was that we *deserved*. However, this seemed to be a popular approach, even among Bible-believing Christians. Fortunately, our consistent approach in using Scripture alone truly allowed us to steer clear of false doctrine or prosperity teaching. Aside from prayer, we really found that we had to encourage our children to do what they enjoy. One of my sons shared:

I don't ever recall a moment or situation in which I was expected to do something because Dad said I had to or Mom gave me no other choice (in respect to extracurricular activities or hobbies, that is). I was always encouraged to pursue what interested me, and in that, was always encouraged to do it to the best of my abilities. I was not a football player. I was a band student. Regardless, I was supported and encouraged to seek out these avenues and to do them with excellence, irrespective of what my brother or sister decided to engage in.

Dinnertime was always a time of lively conversation, learning, exploration, challenge, encouragement, discipline, and laughter—five nights a week. My son recently shared, "The simple act of having dinner together as a family proved a small pillar of consistency that stood the test of time, holding steadfast through the berating storms of financial strife, dissolved business endeavors, careers gained and lost, and numerous other life circumstances." In a recent conversation with him, he shared how he specifically recalled memories as a child having to eat dinner well after seven one evening because his dad was working a job that didn't allow him to get home until late. These late-night dinners at that time didn't make much sense to him then, but now thinking about it, he recalled how glad he was that we waited for Dad to come home. The practice of eating together, regardless of how late, instilled a sense of respect in him for his father and subtly reminded him to honor the sacrifice that my husband made when he had to work. The conversations that were had around the dinner table have shaped him and his own children. He shared, "Thinking back, I can distinctly remember when I was able to begin having 'intelligent' conversations with my siblings. The dinner topics changed from wanting ice cream, to wondering how ice cream was made, to the economic impacts of ice cream on the local economy, to wanting to know how a politician could turn a conversation about immigration status into an ice cream analogy." Dinnertime, just like date night, is now one of those "protected" times in his own family that he's decided is non-negotiable. Even now, with a four-month-old daughter who doesn't even know what food is, my son and his wife sit together with their daughter at the dinner table every night to share and discuss life together and make decisions.

POWER Reflections:

- Each day, encourage your children and tell them how much you love and believe in them. Pray with them each day. They must know that even if you ever fall out of their lives for any reason, God forbid, the Lord will still remain with them.

- Pray with your children at night before they go to bed—either as a family or individually. Learn the art of caring for your children—anyone can provide food, shelter, and clothing. After all, you can provide those things to a total stranger. But not everyone can honestly care for the well-being of their loved ones through making tough choices, setting ground rules, and sticking to them. Being good parents reaps wonderful benefits in years to come.

- Set a time for family Bible study at least once a week and have discussions after church to determine if your children understand spiritual fundamentals. Check throughout the week during "power of the boardroom" dinner meetings about how they applied these principles.

- Teach your children how to handle adversity in dealing with difficult people. Teach them how to become strategic thinkers and the art of applying biblical reasoning from a position of strength.

CONCLUSION

"What lies behind us and what lies before us are tiny matters compared to what lies within us."
—Henry Stanley Haskins-

"Cast all your fears on Him because He cares for YOU!"
—1 Peter 5:7

Over the years as I progressed in my career, I had to ask myself tough questions. One of the toughest: How does my faith impact my career? Should it? My answer was a surprise and revealed that my truth and my motives weren't as selfless as I had thought. When meeting other women on business trips, regardless of their socioeconomic status, culture, or education, we all agreed that there was enormous complexity in our roles as leaders. Sometimes we wondered if it was worth it. Our lives were multifaceted and demanding. As much as we strived to operate and compete in a man's world, at the end of the day all we valued and yearned for was peace of mind. We found that harmony in our lives was far more rewarding than being defined by our jobs as so often men are. Our careers, no matter how great, paled in comparison to our happiness. If our personal lives were in chaos, we lacked a relationship with our spouse or children, and were not operating from our true divine purpose in life, we had to ask ourselves: What is the point?

I hope reading my story provided a glimpse of how my ambitions, sprinkled with my good intentions, blinded me to the perfect will of God and how I suffered consequences for not putting my faith and family first. Most importantly, I hope that *The Power of the Boardroom* helped you take an honest look inward to understand your true motives for your life and how God plays a role in it. There comes a time when we must stop running like Jonah, obey the voice of God, and say enough is enough.

When drawing our line in the sand as it relates to our faith, some of us believe that our commitment can only be realized in church or in a pulpit. I dare say that this is the greatest fallacy of them all. True Christianity takes place in every aspect of your life, especially in the workplace. I've come to believe that society has a lot to do with what "enough" is and how we define success.

CONCLUSION

Think about how it would feel to shape your priorities around who you are as a follower of Christ. Imagine a recipe for success that had your personal values as the main ingredient, mixed with your intellect, a splash of passion, lightly stirred with moral conviction, and served on the rocks of financial stability. In my own journey, I've made the mistake of defining my success through the lenses of competitors driven to excel and persevere at any cost. I challenge you not to make that same mistake. Life is not a game. It is intermingled with real-life consequences that sometimes cannot be changed. My story is proof that the benefits attained in building a successful career, wealth, and influence cannot happen if you lose yourself in the process. To truly enjoy your purpose in life you can only achieve true victory with your soul intact. Life happens regardless and in spite of your plans, ambitions, wants, and dreams. What happens when life doesn't work out as we planned? If you've constructed a life with *your* truth and not someone else's truth, you can't be defeated when life throws you obstacles. Those obstacles become part of the journey—a welcomed opportunity to learn, grow, and thrive. Accountability for our actions only occurs if we own our decisions from the very beginning. Why take the risk to live your life by man's standards with no guarantees of support, rather than by God's, who has a plethora of testimonials from people who have successfully trusted God and found inner peace?

After experiencing many business and personal setbacks in my quest for success, my journey eventually led to a gradual decline in my physical and emotional health resulting in loss of income and the ability to work, which led to personal bankruptcy. Now, looking back on it, I see why it all happened. I did not realize it at the time, but if I'm honest with myself, I was not prepared to grow and run a profitable business. Even though I had legitimate dreams of making a good living for me and my family by using my God-given talents to work, I could not realize the impact of my selfish motives during this time in my life. My soul wasn't intact and I had lost sight of the woman God designed me to be. I let money drive my goals and desires. I believed my God-given talent was enough to build a successful business. Even though this is partly true, your talent, no matter how great, is a small starting point. The real success lies in your ability to first acknowledge the reason that you were drawn to your career in the first place. Ask yourself, "What's my calling?" A true business leader is a visionary—an innovative and progressive mind who is motivated to help make life better. Secondly, think about how using your divine gifts and talents can produce a positive impact and influence—

possibly globally—to motivate others to walk in their divine purpose. I finally learned that the true secret to personal and professional success is accomplished if your ambitions provide a sense of purpose, peace, and hope. Once I realized this, I was able to adopt a positive outlook on life and accept my circumstances as a gift rather than a punishment. My confidence grew because I became happy with who I was and did not let someone else's opinion of me matter more than who God said that I was in Him as a result of my faith. I was able to restore my career, raise a productive family, and keep my marriage from crumbling. I know my painful journey was especially designed to help shape me into a better wife, mother, and professional.

I hope that sharing a glimpse of my life illustrates the power of encouragement, humility, and hope while showing the importance of creating generational blessings for your family. I am no longer the woman who needs status to feel worthy and victorious. Today, my success can be found in my new approach to balancing life, career, and more importantly, my faith.

I leave you with the task of designing your own wheel of success interconnecting your faith, family, and community with one purpose in mind: to build generational blessings for your family and ultimately for the world. Shift your career ambitions from one of self-centeredness to one of purpose and conviction. Design your boardroom in both your personal and work environments to empower your relationships, your children's lives, and your circle of influence. Know that there is strength in your vision and that as you reach the mountaintop of success—your boardroom—then and only then will you be able to spiritually embrace the love of Christ and decide what success looks like for you and your family for generations to come. Choose wisely and know that you are worth God's best.

ACKNOWLEDGEMENTS

This book is dedicated to all families who understand the power of God's blessing! Thank you to each of my family members and close friends who poured out their love and encouragement, which gave me the courage to tell my story. Your prayers and support have meant the world to me.

Even though I am telling *my* story, the *real* story is about the generational blessings that were bestowed upon my family because of my husband's willingness to model his Christian faith in our home. His obedience helped spark my obedience, which helped spark our children's obedience, and our grandchildren's obedience. The blessings still flow. Thank you, Michael, for steering the ship and helping to create our home. Your leadership and love for the family inspired me to grow as a wife, mother, and businesswoman. If it were not for your love and support, I could not have given myself so freely. Michael, thank you for modeling the meaning of servant leadership, commitment, and sacrificial love.

You helped me realize that real men are godly men who stand up for their families and are committed at all costs. If it were not for your dedication to Christ that inspired you to stand by me when we both had the choice and desire to walk away, we would not be where we are today. So for that sacrifice, my love, I dedicate this book to you—my gentle yet strong and courageous warrior who fought for our family and won!

REQUEST TO MY READERS

Call to Action

Please visit our website at www.rbgbusinesssoltutions.com to share your success stories of how you created your personal and professional boardrooms. Go to info@rbgbiz.com to request speaking engagements and to learn more about our upcoming Power of the Boardroom Conferences!

> *With sincere gratitude,*
> RHONDA B. GAINES

ABOUT THE AUTHOR

Rhonda Gaines, founder and CEO of RBG Business Solutions, LLC is a highly sought-after speaker whose passion for leadership development has helped build a successful career in business, human resources and higher education. While working in the private sector for more than twenty years, Rhonda has led teams in competitive work environments and consistently elevated new benchmarks for improved company performance.

Rhonda's unique work experience in working with small business and in corporations offers a valuable perspective and competitive advantage to her new clients. Her ability to get the "job" done has consistently piqued the interest of national brands such as Texas Instruments, The Walt Disney Company, Verizon Wireless, Bank of America, PSE&G, and Texaco. She is also a dedicated mentor and provides life coaching to top-talent professionals in fields of management and business. Throughout her career, Rhonda has garnered numerous awards and recognitions for her performance and management practices. She lives in Cedar Hill, Texas.

> For more information, contact Rhonda at
> **rhonda@rbgbiz.com.**